And the birds still fly

Pam Rosenblatt

Published by Eden Waters Press
Editor: Anne Brudevold
16 Harcourt St. #2B
Boston, MA 02116

www.edenwaterspress.com
Published in the USA

ISBN-978-0-9825186-3-2

Acknowledgments

Credit:

"To see with the heart" was inspired by
Antoine de Saint-Exupéry's *Le Petit Prince.*

Published poems:

Earlier versions of "Any neighborhood", "daylight savings time" and "On the cottage's roof" [formerly "The birds who coo"] were published in *The Somerville News* (2006), *Bagels with the Bards* – No. 3 (2008), and *Fictionaut* (2010) respectively.

In gratitude:

With appreciation to Kathleen Spivack for her expert writing guidance; Anne Brudevold of Eden Waters Press for publishing *As the birds fly*; Harris Gardner, Linda Larson, and Charlotte Eckler for their editorial suggestions; Steve Glines for his layout recommendations; Karen Duplessis for the cover design; and Mignon Ariel King, proofreader. Thank you to the late George Starbuck, Bonnie Costello, Doug Holder, and Lisa Rosenblatt for their knowledge. My gratitude to all the Bagelbards whose insights and friendships have motivated me to write and publish *And the birds still fly.* And finally, but not least, my sincere thanks to Mark Aicher and my parents for their steady direction throughout this journey. Without all of you, this book would have remained but a manuscript on one of my bookshelves.

Thank you, once again!

To the loving memories

of my grandparents,

Clara and George & Mollie and Simon

There are so many ways to ruin a poem
it's quite amazing good ones ever get written.

—John Berryman, 1954

Contents

Questions of Poetry

Is it true a poem isn't a poem until there's a word until there's a phrase until there's a sentence until there's a structure until there's rhythm until there's meter until there's imagery until there's metaphor until there's emotion? Or until someone reasons that this run-on is accurate? What if a poem is just a run-on sentence, just one repetition or more than one repetition, just reality eclipsed into imagination, just word play, just emotion. Who is to say what makes a poem a poem anyway? Does a poem need punctuation and capital letters to be called "poetry"? Does a poem have to rhyme? Does a poem have to meet certain criteria? Does a poem have to look a specific way? After all, once such a poem is composed, completed, defined, the birds still fly!

Prelude

The night

One day, the night falls –
Like the water over Niagara.
The woman sees, runs to catch it,
But the summer darkness seeps
Through her fingers. It doesn't
Go splat, all just shines black.

Then, she sees, goes for a shooting star,
Accidently in her hands catches two mating fireflies,
Soon releases them to do their thing.
Next, she eyes the Big, Little Dippers,
The Milky Way, wonders what the Dippers hold,
If it's possible to unwrap the abstracted candy bar.

Her hands reach towards the Dippers, the Milky Way,
Capture floating dandelion fluff instead.
She sits, cross-legged, on the ground,
'Til the campfire dwindles,
The moon slips down behind the field,
The sun eases itself up over the trees.

Identity Crisis

What is she?

What is she is she is she
but a body sitting on a
faux leather chair inside
an old bedroom revamped
into the woman's office, typing
on the keyboard's keys of
a multi-year old computer
still priding itself on XP and not Vista,
waiting for a friend, relative,
foe to call on the white pushbutton land line

phone resting on the Formica-
covered slab of wood that
lies on top of two two-door
file cabinets filled with old
cash receipts and books
not yet published and lots
and lots of desk accessories
like tape, pens, pencils, floppy
disks. Once upon a time she was
organized, or, what she means to
say, her desk drawers and her
office in general was a more
structured space. But that was before
life's everyday distractions took
toll. Dictionaries – English, Spanish,
French, German – and poetry books –
Jorie Graham, Langston Hughes,
Elizabeth Bishop, Jane Shore, Charles
Bukowski and more – and miscellaneous
books randomly pack the shelves of her pine
bookcase. On a rectangular table rests
a printer that's waiting, yearning to be plugged in,
turned on, and used for black-white color printing. Why is
she here in this room and not out in the den or the kitchen or the laundry
room? She doesn't have a deadline to meet. She doesn't have emails to answer.
She's just typing. She doesn't have anything to do except clean up this place scattered
with papers and library books on the floor – and she'll tend to that chore once she's figured
out why is she what is she what   is she what is she is she...

Dreams

Did you ever...dream?

Did you, the chorus, ever catch a toad
And wish it could fly, much like
A monarch butterfly?

Once caught a toad and let it go.

Did you, the chorus, ever hold a snake
And let it slither away,
Through some uncut grass?

Once held a snake and freed it in newly mowed grass.

Did you, the chorus, every build a sandcastle
And wish it were real,
Much like an English manor?

Once built a sandcastle and let the incoming tide do its thing.

Did you, the chorus, ever dig a hole
But only get sore arms?

Once dug a hole so deep that water seeped in.

Did you, the chorus, ever see a firefly,
And chase it with a bottle or a net,
Never to grasp the bug in your hands?

Once raced for a lightning bug that disappeared into the sky.

Did you, the chorus, ever dream a dream of a dream
And wake still in a dream, never
To forget that a dream is only a dream?

Huh?

To see with the heart

The woman has two eyes, both blue, but would rather
See things with the heart... How 'bout you?
To look at the clouds, the sky, the moon, and the sun
Is grand, yes! But she would rather see things with the heart.

To see the oceans' waves, the lakes' winds, and the rivers' flows
Is wonderful, indeed. But she would rather see things with the heart.
To view the daisies, the sunflowers, and the marigolds is special,
Just like their perfumes. But she would rather see things with the heart.

It's simple to look through eyes. Open. Shut.
Things are just there. To look with the heart is more of an art.
To find a little prince atop a mountain's peak or Asteroid B-612's Crater
Has more appeal when visualized with the heart –

A postcard, a book, a movie –
Visual yet understood only
when you let the heart in.

To you, the chorus, may you always see things with your heart –
Let compassion, emotion beat steadily through.

Where did you go?

The woman opens a kitchen window,
In twirls a many-colored feathered animal.
She jumps, closes the window.
The strange being retraces its flight, hits the cold glass.
Boom! Down goes the provocative thing.

Then, the silent creature suddenly awakes, oscillates
Its broad wings. The woman rushes to, re-opens the window.
Out of the house, into the backyard, it pirouettes, spins.
Colors red-blue-green-yellow-orange blend together
Like an extra-large scoop of rainbow ice cream.

Her eyes blink; she shuts the window.
When odd-shaped plumaged ballerinas materialize,
Doing jigs, jags, pirouettes on barren tree branches.

Her husband walks in, simply says,
    What are you doing?
She replies,
    Watching birds outside the window.
He pushes up the window, moves,
Looks from side to side, asks,
    What birds?
He tries to catch a glimpse, says,
    There's nothing there except the setting sun,
    Some trees and the autumn lawn.
He walks away.

She glances outside, shrugs.
Her face flushes from a wind burst.

She looks down, sees there, on the window sill,
A red-blue-green-yellow-orange quill tremble,
Caught between some loose pieces of peeling white paint.

Fantasies without caring

Zits she has zits all over her...
Boyfriends she has boyfriends all over her...
Not slander she has not slander all over her...
What does it matter?

Rolls of fat she has rolls of fat all over her...
Boyfriends she has boyfriends all over her...
Not slander she has not slander all over her...
What does it matter?

It's like their inner dreams are brought to surface...
They act out their fantasies without caring about whom they hurt...
They don't listen to others underneath or on top...
What does it matter?

Psychologists, psychiatrists, social workers say,
Nice. They have nice written all about them...
Others smile. They had others smile at them...
Call the police, some think. *Call the police!*

But then the psychologists, psychiatrists, social workers say,
How are you feeling? Are you feeling?
The answer is a smile and a shrug of the shoulders...
She is a photographer, a writer, a friend, unwilling to compete

With their vivid world of escapism, at least anymore...

That one, she swears, has zits she has zits all over her...
Boyfriends she has boyfriends all over her...
Not slander she has not slander all over her...
What does it matter?

That other one has rolls of fat she has rolls of fat all over her...
Boyfriends she has boyfriends all over her...
Not slander she has not slander all over her...
What does it matter? Does it matter

That they are all part of the same system?

It matters! The woman thinks, *It matters!*

Out of darkness

Out of darkness come
Dreams, dreamers of dreams,
Prophets and God-fearing people.

Look at Abimelekh and his Holy dream
Keeping him "innocent" with "clean hands"[1] –
Just return Abraham's wife, Sarah, originally
Thought to be only the prophet's sister.
Fear God enough and good things may happen.
Look at Laban the Aramaean and his Holy dream
Warning him not to say negative or positive things
To Jacob about his actions of leaving Laban's land
Without saying "goodby"[2] and taking Laban's children
Away without a hug or a kiss.
In other words, fear God enough and good things
Will happen – like the symbolic treaty
Called "Witness Mound" or "Gal'ed"[3].
Look at Joseph and his two Holy dreams about his brothers' bundles
Making a circle around and kowtowing to Joseph's upright cluster
And about the sun and the moon and eleven stars "bowing
Down" to the younger brother.[4]
In other words, fear God enough and good things
May come to you, even lead
To the reign of a land like Egypt
And all because of dreams that made his older
Brothers jealous enough to sell him into slavery.

Yes, out of darkness comes
Dreams, dreamers of dreams,
Prophets and God-fearing people.

1 Rabbi Aryeh Kaplan, The Living Torah : The Five Books of Moses and The Haftarot. New York: Maznaim Publishing Corporation, 1981, p. 89
2 Ibid, p.149.
3 Ibid, p.149.
4 Ibid, p. 185

Neighborhoods

Any neighborhood

The boy across the street
Skateboards night and day.
Wheels turn on the cement
And screech to halts.
Sometimes wood scrapes
The sidewalk or driveway.

The elderly man down the street
Sweeps his sidewalk every day.
Swish. Swish. The yellow straw broom
Slips, slides. The fallen buds,
Turned leaves and small broken branches
All neatly piled in tiny batches.

The carpenter on the roof a few houses away
Yanks at, throws old nails and battered tiles down
Below on the green-brown grass.
Then, the electric stapler gun punches nails into new tiles
Into the roof. The mess on the ground is thrown
Into dark green trash bags while the roof,
Tile by tile, is quickly put together
Rain clouds speed the process.

The red SUV pulls out of a driveway with children
Piling into it through the open sliding door.
The door shuts, and the car drives away,
Quickly and silently.

Finally, an apartment

1. this white stucco
needs a coat of paint or two
before autumn ends

and winter time arrives
squirrels play in the gutters

2 potted marigolds
hang from brown wooden railings
next to the stairway

where the landlord stands smiling
and waving to the woman

3. antiquated door
opens and leads to new world
foreign, strange to her

old-fashioned wooden staircase
with a wooden banister

4. renter in bright garb
asks them to take off shoes,
in respect for Allah

covered feet feel the bare floor
a kitten runs past her and purrs

5. worn wooden floors
with cracks in some of the planks
her socks' bottoms catch,

tear since no wooden filler
has set in the crevices

6. the kitchen flooring
found here in this abode
ancient blue and white

reminds the woman of her
grandparents' kitchen floor pattern

7. the kitchen's wall tile
is blue and looks antique
which it should because it is

the entire two-family
house is one hundred years old

8. what a grand space
a living room, dining room
two bedrooms and a study

all with off-white painted walls
high ceilings and wooden fans

9. outside backyard
weedy flower, vegetable
beds with a mature gray fence

surrounding them, a green lawn
in the center of the yard

10. green and purple grapes
fill the white wicker baskets
on a clothed table

a scene solely for today
butterflies fly near the fruit

11. the landlord shakes her hand,
closes the gate's door as he exits,
drives away in a corolla

his shoes leave behind
footprints on the green grass

About what green is...

The woman is at her desk, looks at her computer monitor,
Finds website links linking "Somerville" with word
"Green", finds green!

Is Somerville turning green? Is the Green Line extension really
Coming to this fair city? Is the pollution from I-93, route 128,
And other major main roads shouldering the brunt of local traffic
Ever going to go away?

Is green going to root itself in Somerville with its colors green?

Is the city exploring green vehicles with biodiesel fuel for Somerville
A way to cut down on the thousands spent per year on city pollution?

Is the mixed green salad with cherry tomatoes, cucumbers, red onions
And French feta cheese with balsamic dressing for fewer than ten dollars
Worth it at Orleans restaurant in Davis Square?

Is Union Square's India Palace's green aloo mutter, or fresh green peas made with
Potatoes and spices and herbs tasty, worth the just over ten dollars cost?

Is Davis Square's Spark Craft Studios' hunter green awning
Decorated with white letters just green because it's a nice color green?

On another note, why is the word "green" so clean, so lively, so popular? And why
Did she want to write a "green" environmental poem for this Bagelbard reading?
And does it matter that "green" has been her favorite color since childhood anyway?

For a Change, a Danish

One March morning
The woman exits from Harvard Square's
Au Bon Pain holding a white paper bag.
A young man walks up to her
And asks for change.

His breath is but white smoke in the air.
She doesn't want to give him money,
But does want to hand him the warm
Pastry inside that white paper bag.
He doesn't know her; she doesn't know him.

All they both know is she had just walked
Out of that Cambridge café when
Their eyes met. She gives him that wrinkled
Paper bag. He looks at her, says, *Thank you.*
Then she heads toward a MBTA bus stop,

Glances behind her, sees him sitting down
On the dirty snow-covered sidewalk,
Eating his pastry. Near him, people smoke,
Drink from coffee cups, or place one foot
In front of the other on their way to wherever.

She pulls her hat over her head,
Closes her coat tightly. The bus arrives.
She steps aboard, takes some quarters
Out of her change purse, drops
Them into the meter's money slot.

In her study

She gazes out the window again.
The cumulus have somehow connected,
Turned gray. Thunder rolls with
A sharp strike of white-yellow across
The smoke-hued sky. Minutes later,
Sheep-shaped clouds, Hawaiian blue
Streak across the sky.

Something bangs, falls, makes a loud sound
From the apartment downstairs. Golden
Rays burst between spaces of clouds and sky.

It's April's end, and she longs to see
The full-chested pigeon return to its
Perch on the triangular tip of the neighbor's
Roof, but it won't happen today.

A plane whirs over head. The TV with
Its subtle music fills the apartment.

The woman's fingers tap the keyboard.
Good, her fingers move smoothly, efficiently.
Soon she rises from the chair, turns the plastic rod around
Until the white shade's slats close out the dulling light.

Nature

Her wild life

1: The gray-white squirrel

Along the wooden backyard fence, a gray-white squirrel races, leaps,
Jumps onto a weak tree branch, hops back onto the fence, then
Goes onto a sloping bough, loses grasp, plunges downward
Onto the brush, stone, dirt below. It lands on the right side of its body,

Struggles to right itself. It exerts, rests, exerts again.
A wide wing-spanned bird circles overhead, flies away.
The gray-white squirrel moves onto its stomach,
Then struggles towards the neat lawn.

The bird returns, does a 360. The squirrel pulls itself up, turns around,
Hesitates, drags itself into the brush, dirt near corner where the fence and
The back of the garage meet. The stalker swoops down.
The gray-white squirrel hasn't been seen for days.

2: The large cat

The bright just-turned-on garage overhead light
Illuminates the darkened backyard, especially the newly
Tilled garden filled with fresh green seedlings, especially

The large whiskered yellow-white cat looks
Over at the vegetables' greenery then at the woman,
And takes off faster than a shock from a broken power line.

How graceful, quick is this animal of the wild.
How curious a look does it give before
Charging into the next door neighbor's backyard.

3: The dazed raccoon

The messy black-gray raccoon swaggers
In the road. The afternoon summer
Rays add to the heated, dazed look in its
Black eyes. The car's horn breaks the silence,

The raccoon sways then steps on its front paws.
Her eyes stare. The car stops on the road's edge.
The cell phone's buttons beep
As the 911 call is dialed.

4: The unfazed opossum

The white prickly furred, pink-skinned
Tailed opossum isn't noticed at first
By the woman and her purple

Leashed pet walking stop-and-go,
On the newly cemented sidewalk,
In the silent morning neighborhood.

They start to move more quickly, with
The dog's paws, the owner's feet
In sync, when the noiseless night dweller

Crosses the street, takes a shortcut,
Right across their path. The startled pair
Continue walking, look a long time at

The rude animal, as such behavior
Isn't customary for that side of the street!
This is such a silly scene to an elderly man

Who has just raised a window shade in a nearby
Cottage. The unfazed opossum hurries to a front
Yard, away from the pair, into not far away brush.

Through her mind's eye: the Moultonborough connections

There are connections that have been around in
The woman's mind's eye for over thirty years –
With sightings of deer, bear, raccoons, skunks, squirrels,
Humming birds, woodpeckers, blackbirds, robins, seagulls,

Perch, bass – lots and lots of bass. There have been trees –
Spruces, maples, elms and, recently, losses of lots of
Spruces, maples, elms. And flowers – wild buttercups,
Petunias, marigolds, and more marigolds.

And vegetables – tomatoes and more tomatoes.
There have been tornadoes, rainstorms, snowstorms,
Windstorms, no storms, sunshine, moonshine,
Clouds – cirrus, stratus, cumulonimbus – and no clouds.

There's been planet watching and star gazing.
Dark skies and blue skies. Gray sunsets. Orange-red sunsets.
Campfires and cookouts. Burgers and hot dogs. Lobsters and
Corn on the cob. Cole slaw. Potato salad. Potato chips.

Marshmallows cooked over an open flame. And s'mores made
With burnt marshmallows, Hershey's milk chocolate
Between two graham crackers. There's been sunbathing on the beach.
Kayaking, canoeing, boat rides, waterskiing, swimming, in the Lake.

And people, lots and lots of people, numbers growing every summer.
There's been weekend and week-long visits to her folks' camp.
Dinners, lunches, brunches at relatives' and neighbors' homes.
And there have been walks from the Lake to the country store

And back home for newspapers, groceries, and mosquito repellent.
And there's been tennis for fun on a cement tennis court with a green
Wooden backboard attached to a silver metal fence. And golf, lots
And lots of golf with relatives and friends.

The connections are all here – in this poem, in her mind's eye,
In Moultonborough, New Hampshire.

In her dining room

Varnished green purple red grapes
Push against each other falling over
The chubby chipped red-hued apple and
Two portly peeling lime-colored pears all tucked
Inside the dark wood bowl planted centered
On top of the tan oilclothed cherry table
With four matching wooden chairs
Fruit too hard to consume
Scene easy to photograph.

The porch bench

Hot rays color

Half the porch bench;
The other half shaded by
The

Gray

White

Vertically

Striped

Awning.

A six-legged insect constructs
A translucent home –
On the bench's
Lower right leg.

A spotted-black yellow winged creature
Lingers, flutters overhead.

It's late morning,
The spring breeze wafts.

The straw broom pushes pollen, dead bugs,
Twigs from under the bench into a nearby pile.

The birds

1. The bird of flutter

Minute sun yellow bird

With rapid, stirring wings

Hovers, drinks

Lilac's nectar.

Oh, how his wings fan

Endlessly,

Spectators' eyes

Tire.

Funny, huh, how

Such painterly attributes

Catch interests.

2. On the cottage's roof

Purple-gray short-winged
Birds with awkward, bobbing heads.
Pale ash color feet, gray beaks
Clatter against chipped wood gray roof tiles.
Coos, coos echo in the spring air.
Their caviar-hued eyes stare at
The silver container banded to their right / left legs.
They are owned, yet take to cloudless blue.
It's flight time now!
Deliver messages,
Journey back.
They for
Are live
The who
Homing pigeons
Destiny.

3. Flights

Two orange-red-bellied robins sport gray bodies, wings.
Gritty beaks yank thick brown-pink worms from muddy burrows
Below spring grass. Naturally shiny heads shake, jiggle such ambushed.

Wings flap. Full-mouthed birds run through
Blades of recently mowed runway,
Lift off, soar toward cumulus.

Flights level, land home – dried mud, twigs,
Browned grass – on a tree branch.
Three yellowish chirpers feed,

Jump out. Elders watch shaky take-offs,
Fly after them, head for another seasonal lawn,
Other worms to catch.

Chaos

daylight savings time

today's daylight savings time and of course she forgot to change the clocks last night so when she woke up at 6 am she said go away to the alarm clock but got up anyway today is important she has to shop for holiday presents so she got up out of bed and washed up and ate and looked at her cell phone its automatic clock read 5:15 am holy moley she forgot its daylight savings time she guesses she already saved time today.

Computer chaos

There's a poem in this, the woman thinks, as she waits on the phone.
What's she to do? She makes some hot tea, eats some grapes,
Munches on cookies and still, minutes later, is waiting.

Where's human contact – any human contact?

Her PC is only three months old, and the six prior phone calls to
computer technical support haven't prevented relapses. Each time
the hold button has been on for a long, long time.

Today's no different, no different at all.

A half of an hour passes. Another twenty minutes goes by. Then
A British accented voice interrupts the digital music playing in
Her ear, *Hello, I'm So N. So. Can I have your first, last name, then*
Your computer serial number?

She gives the man the information and thinks, *Wow! My voice is probably*
In India or China or Korea or Israel. How amazing!

The voice says, *What is the computer problem?*
She says, *It just doesn't work anymore. I think it crashed.*
The voice says, *No problem, we can fix it....*

And he dictates directions to her, gains computer screen access,
Then puts her call on hold.

Twenty minutes later, the voice says, *Everything's set.*
She chomps loudly on a cookie, calmly says, *Can I return the computer?*
It's broken seven times, and I bought it only three months ago.
The voice says, *I'm so sorry, but the 30 day warrantee has passed.*

The woman finishes the cookie, hangs up the phone.
What can she do? What if the computer breaks again?
Why did the world advance beyond the quill and ink?
The manual typewriter? The electric typewriter?

Why did man have to invent the phone's digital voice and music?

Maybe computers are actually world rulers,
Along with the assistance of computer technicians!

Oh how intellectually superior to people are these machines,
But everyday stresses always do them in. Like when they break down.
Human intelligence is needed to repair them. Or when the machines
become outdated? Human intelligence is again required.

And oh how chaos strikes when computers go awry.
But presently, the chaos converts to the sublime –
And her computer works once more!
Now to reboot...

The apple tree

It's like the woman sees the apples fall far
From the tree, get bruised, worm-holed, and ant-eaten.

Yes, it's like the fruit never ripen
To their full saturated red hue, only green
With speckles of yellow-orange.

There are lots of trees in this neighborhood.
With lots of houses, too, for that matter.

And lots of cars and lots of people
And lots and lots of dogs on leashes –
Well, most of them on leashes. And squirrels,

Well, they dart and zigzag across the faded
Gray asphalt side of the street. But who cares?

For the apple she's glaring at fell far from the tree,
A tree which is still dangling with holed
Apple ornaments. And it took just one old

Man to take his Beebe gun and shoot at
This sprouting old McIntosh tree. Bang.

The neighbors hear. The squirrels
Run around on the ground as erratically
As the sparrows, crows, hawks that fly

In the cloudy gray sky. Why, oh why, do the
Neighbors shrug, continue on their paths

Heading to and from work, gardening,
Bringing in groceries day after day after day?
The neighborhood police car drives slowly

By the tree several times a day, with the old man
Just waving his hand in friendly gestures.

The woman doesn't stop her routine
To speak with the young officers.
She just continues writing

While the apples fall far from the tree, bruised,
Worm-holed, ant-eaten, Beebe-bearing.

Yes, it's like the fruit never ripen to
Their full saturated red hue, only green
With speckles of yellow-orange. Each day,

The old man shoots his gun at this tree. Each day,
The neighbors hear, shrug, continue on their paths.

Those poor apples lie on the grass, the sidewalk,
The street, never to be consumed, never to find
Their way into a pie.

Why is the old man winning? Is he winning?

And the birds still fly...

Phase I: metrowest boston

it snowed all yesterday and last night. the oil-heated radiators
warmed this hundred year old italian stucco house. a wet, white
flannel blanket with squirrel paw prints spread upon the neighborhood:
the so still houses, the not long yards, the sharp inclining driveways,
the wheel imprinted street. today, the neighborhood's alive with shovels
scraping against iced, snowed pavements and with the sputtering
of sand shooting plows on the slushy, beige-black-white road.

Phase II: haiti

it quaked last january. land shook, cracked, dropped.
buildings fell down plop, communications disrupted.
the injured, scared, confused, lost mourning loved ones
walked the broken streets in the stark winter caribbean heat.

Phase III: haiti

what a natural, beautiful place you once were and
will be again. how much the world wants to be there,
comfort you, and assist you through this time of trouble.
may you rebuild, become stronger, overcome mother earth's
grumblings, rants, and raves, overcome the fears instilled
so suddenly by uneven movements of earth's plates.

Phase IV: haiti

it happened centuries before and you grew again,
though poverty and disease have overpowered.

Phase V: haiti

how mother nature and mother earth
sometimes work in twisted, inconceivable ways –
sometimes wondrous; sometimes awful.
how minute mankind is amidst such forces.

Phase VI: world

this winter jolt affected most everyone. caring eyes,
supporting actions from everywhere answered
mother nature's and mother earth's powerful calls.
yet were and are the energies generated worth the while?

Phase VII: haiti

the earth quaked last january. land shook, cracked, dropped.
buildings fell down plop, communications disrupted.

Phase VIII: metrowest boston

and the skies snowed all yesterday and last night. the oil-heated
radiators warmed this one hundred year old italian stucco house.

Peace as...

She is like...

A sparrow

A robin

A blue jay

Flying

About

Spring's greenery,

Enjoying

The season

But probably

Not the path

Of Nature –

For that isn't predictable, peaceful.

Jellyfish

Clear, jiggly, round with pink tentacles,
Hug sea and sand-worn stones
Embedded on the neighborhood beach.
Several children in bathing suits throw
Rocks at the captive sea creatures.
Some poke the jellyfish with sticks.
A teenage, freckled boy picks up a
Horseshoe crab by its front stick
And flings it back into the shallow
Ocean. No swimming today.
The jellyfish have invaded.

Chain letter – from the IRS

A chain letter email! The woman just received
A chain letter email indirectly
From the IRS. A friend of a friend
Works for the IRS and forwarded
This chain letter to her.
So what, you say. *Chain letters*
Come and chain letters go.
But, she replies, *This isn't your typical IRS*
Chain letter emailed document.
What is it? you ask.
Well, it's kind of a journalistic poem with
Photographs and alternating
Lines of isolationist theory plus
Lines of war reality testing.
The photos are touching –
American soldiers crying,
Never changing their clothes,
Petting a kitten in a war zone,
While all the time the Americans at home
Just go on their merry ways of
Watching TV, shopping,
Complaining about getting the wrong
Meal at a restaurant
How can this be?
Our country's soldiers are on strange
Foreign lands, thinking about dying, saving
The lives of people – there and in America!
It's a political jargon piece filled
With words, photos, emotional play.
Who is right? Who is wrong?

Should the United States put their men
And women, though trained for the situations
Confronted, in those situations?
Should the United States relieve
The soldiers of their war responsibilities,
Send them home to be with family, friends?
Should anyone view such violence on a daily basis?
Shouldn't the people of the world just live in
Happy, prosperous times instead
Of death, destruction?

A chain letter email! The woman just received a
Chain letter email indirectly from the government –
Err...The IRS. And it totally opened both eyes
With opposing perspectives happening at the same time!
Go America! Go Soldiers! Go Away WARS.

What will happen if she doesn't respond?
Maybe she'll send out just one chain letter email.

Just one....

Tears.

Tears drip out from her swollen
Tear ducts, very slowly, one at
A time. Like droplets of
Soda edgily sliding down
A bottle of pop. She doesn't
Even wipe the tears from
Her cheeks. She just types.
Why is this happening?
Where? Why?
When did the wrongs
Originate? How
Did everything
Change so profoundly?
Why did the people
Make the switch from
Conservative to radical?
From stable to erratic?
From healthy to unstable?
How come people change?
How come people aren't
Accepting people, individuals,
With their varying philosophies,
Tastes, social, economic backgrounds?

Chaos seems to be in vogue –
Lots, lots of chaos. She doesn't
Understand. All she wants is
To write and live her life
Without having to wipe
The tears from her cheeks.
To just let them roll down
'Til they fall from her face
Land on the desktop,
With a splat, gently
Wiped away by a hand
No longer typing
The poems that people
So wanted to read, to hear,
To understand. She is human.
She has tears. She feels them,
Sees them fall, escape.
Please know that, now.

Hello friends

The open white cabinet door reveals shelves abundant:
Unsharpened pencils; plastic blue, black, red ink pens;
Silver paperclips; unopened packages of tape,
Yellow-lined legal pads; manila file folders;
Even CDs and DVD-Rs.

The woman closes the door, touches a yellowed photo,
Its corners taped to the front of the Formica door.
Her lips close, droop downwards. She rests in a faux leather chair.

It's been awhile, dear friends, she muses. It's been decades.
Oh, how the three of us must have changed, grown.

She thinks about how photogenic he was, the young man in the photo.
Now his manly thinness has probably become a bit chubbier.
Well, no – she decides – he must be about the same weight.
But, his once thick, lively blond hair must now be thinner, whiter –
She pictures him and his wife, her college roommate, still married
With two children – probably two boys with the same warm grin
That their father had as an undergrad.

But now, she wonders, *What is he like now? Is he an attorney?*
A professor? A Saint? He was always an athlete, always jogging
With his girlfriend, his wife-to-be, her college roommate.

She remembers that first year of college in Chicago. The three of
Them always doing things together, especially going to campus
Parties, movies, sport events. She is always the third wheel.
Her two friends don't mind. But she does.

The woman smiles, speaks to the aging photograph,
Remember us three eating Häagen Dazs at the local ice cream shop
downtown. Do you remember? And do you remember the time
when you two purchased to extra-large gumballs and tried to put them
into your mouths – unsuccessfully, though?

Then she flashes back to junior year in college when
She transfers to a college in her home state. Winter arrives,
And she returns for a short visit to Chicago.
The threesome travel through the windy city, eat pizza, reminisce.

And to the summer after college graduation – when she travels from
Massachusetts to her friends' hometown in that golden bridge state,
Sees them marry in such a wonderful white-steepled church.

And to the reception, oh, how the groom's face dances
As he guides his bride along on the smooth wooden floor.

Then there's another flashback. The woman looks at the photograph
Her friends pose near a clear glass building. She shuts her eyes.

It is only a few weeks later, in autumn, when the woman
Again journeys to the cosmopolitan city, wonders, *Why am I doing this?*
Coming back here after settling securely in Boston. And it is windy outside.

Multi-colored leaves swirl just above the cement sidewalk,
Mini-tornadoes in the fading evening's light. Inside a rented apartment
The friends dine on Chinese appetizers, bursts of sunshine amidst
The billowing wind. They talk about this, about that.

Then night falls, and the next day the three friends wake up late.
The wind's still spritely. The man goes to work; his wife walks her poodle.

Alone, the woman opens up her suitcase, takes out, puts on
A custom-fitted pair of waxed wings. She raises the window,
Steps toward the noontime sun.

Then the woman stops, coughs, opens her eyes.
Her wings are gone. She twirls around in the faux leather chair,
Her feet stop the chair in front of the white cabinet.
The photograph shines brightly.

She blinks, thinks how wind storms pass into nothingness eventually.
She smiles, removes it from the white cabinet's door.

Be good, bad guy

How do you stop the bad guy, the guy who
Appears sweet, innocent, from hurting

Life – humans and animals in particular?
You – everyone – may, understand underneath

What the bad guy is up to but can never prove
It actually happened on top – for one reason or another.

It's a question, a poem to write. You'll probably never
Get the accurate answer, or the words published.
What? Call the police, you say? You would but

They can't do anything for the bad guy is bad to
The core. The good police are probably afraid,
Would say there's not enough evidence.

(The bad guy probably has friends, if you know what I mean.)

Talk to the bad guy personally? But that probably
Wouldn't help as he she would deny everything.
Tell others out loud how bad the bad guy is?

But that would get back to him her with
More badness from the bad guy as a result.
How do you end this jigsaw puzzle/poem when

The last two to seven pieces/lines are missing?
Perhaps you have an answer; perhaps not.
Guess you'll have to sit back in your leather chair,

Get up the strength to call the police...Or perhaps not.
All you can do is wish for Impossible, hope for Possible
Maybe the bad guy turns good, asks the law, the victims

And the gods for forgiveness, hope, and understanding.
But the gods are known to be wrathful and vengeful, so
The bad guy is unlikely to repent.

Oh well, what a predicament, what a complicated,
Never-ending checkers game where the bad guy is always
Jumping the good guy, cornering his or her victim, who is

Unable to get those cherished checkers kinged and win
Control of the board, the game, justice.

Be good, bad guy, be good. That's about all we can say.
Be good, bad guy. Please be good.

peace as...

The woman reads the newspaper before her
and sees articles about the presidential race
and the iraq war and casually thinks peace as
possible throughout the world if only people
would listen to the calls of peace from the
soldiers, the grandfathers, the fathers, the sons,
the grandmothers, the mothers, the daughters,
and not just the politicians who mean well but
sometimes see color red in hopes of peace as
an end to terrorism. what she means to say is
was mccain right in 2002 when he envisioned war
to get peace in a land that terrorized terrorizes our
own land? he warned and is now coming to view
the iraq war as "mismanaged" and thinks repairs
need to be made to correct to achieve victory in
a land that now deserves peace as what clinton now
wants although she too first thought in 2002 troops
were needed to prevent mass destruction and protect
the united states and she now views the authorization
of troops into iraq as "no longer relevant" and supports
a total troop exodus back to the u.s. and peace as possible
perhaps to obama who since 2002 always voted against
u.s. forces to go into iraq. but who knows the best way
to achieve peace as in a war that can be compared to
vietnam? look at john lennon, golda maier, mother teresa,
joan of arc, all peace advocates in a world craving peace as...
who is right? and who is left? and will war ever be
peace as peace as peace as...

Fonts:
Golden Normal; Golden Bold; Lucida Grande Regular;
Lucida Grande Bold; Nanumunga Bold

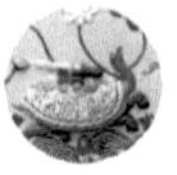

Eden Waters Press

About Pam Rosenblatt

Pam Rosenblatt has written poetry since childhood. She became a published author in 2009 with *On How to Read – THE MANUAL* (Ibbetson St. Press), her first chapbook. Pam is also an editor, poetry reviewer, and visual arts reporter. She has published writings in Bagels with the Bards: *Bagelbard Anthologies II, III, IV, V* (Ibbetson St. Press, 2007, 2008, 2009, 2010); Boston Area Small Press and Poetry Scene; Eden Waters Press Anthologies *Home* and *Journey; Fictionaut; NewsBlaze.com; Small Press Review; The Somerville News;* and *Wilderness House Literary Review.*

www.ingramcontent.com/pod-product-compliance
Ingram Content Group UK Ltd.
Pitfield, Milton Keynes, MK11 3LW, UK
UKHW041839200726
13854UKWH00003BA/1212